This book belongs to
_____

Bible Memory Verse Guide © 2019 by Banyan Tree Publishing
All rights reserved. No part of this book may be used or
reproduced in any manner whatsoever without written
permission except in the case of brief quotations embodied in
critical articles and reviews.
First edition: 2019

# Reasons to Memorize Scripture

One of the best-known and most extensive Biblical writings about the importance of knowing and internalizing the word of God can be found in Psalm 119. Within, the psalmist expresses his love for God through his treasuring of God's written word. He describes how through scripture, God speaks to him, nourishing his soul, guiding his footsteps and broadening his understanding.

To commit God's word to memory is to equip ourselves to face life's joys and challenges with courage and confidence, knowing that God's promises, instructions and truths have been internalized and act as a guide in our daily lives.

## Tips for Selecting Memory Passages

Bible memorization is most effective when you choose verses or passages that have practical relevance in your daily life. Choose passages that:

- Are commonly referred to
- Help fight disbelief or discouragement
- Express gratitude in all circumstances
- Remind you to relinquish your burdens
- Declare God's promises
- Help you focus on the good news of salvation through Jesus Christ

# Tips for Memorizing Scripture

- Make Bible memory a regular part of your daily routine
- Select passages that are personally relevant
- Take the time to study more deeply with the help of various translations, concordances or commentaries
- Reflect on what you have learned and how the passage applies to you
- Find a Bible memory partner to keep you accountable
- Post the passage where you will see it regularly
- Use daily routines like driving, cooking or exercising to recite the passage by memory
- Use actions or mental images to help you "see" the words in your mind
- Break the passage into 5 parts to learn over the course of a week
- Use your hand to help you memorize the full passage. The first part of the passage is associated with your thumb. Recite that portion with a thumbs up. The second part of the passage is associated with your index finger. Touch your index finger to your thumb whenever you recite the second portion, and so on.

# How to Use the Memory Aid

Step 1: Select the passage according to the tips provided.

Step 2: Write the scripture reference and the full memory passage on the next page.

Step 3: Do a deep reading of the passage by referring to a second translation or paraphrase and a concordance or commentary.

Step 4: Reflect on what you have learned on the passage and its relevance to your life or the life of those around you.

Step 5: Set memorization goals and use the finger touching technique to break the passage into easily memorized portions.

Step 6: Use the memory tips provided in this book to commit the passage to your permanent memory by regular review.

Scripture
Reference_____

Write the passage below:

Research Resources

Insights from second translation or paraphrase:

Key words in their original language with their definitions:

Notes from the commentary:

**Reflection**

Why have you chosen to memorize this passage?

_____

_____

What is God saying to you personally through this passage?

_____

_____

_____

_____

_____

_____

In what type of circumstances would knowing this passage
by heart be useful?

_____

_____

_____

_____

## Setting Goals for Memorization

Start Date:

_____

End Date:

_____

Daily Routines to Link to Memorization:

1._____
2._____
3._____

## Memorization Technique

Divide the passage into 5 parts, one part for each finger. Write each portion of the passage beside the finger you will touch when reciting that part of the passage.

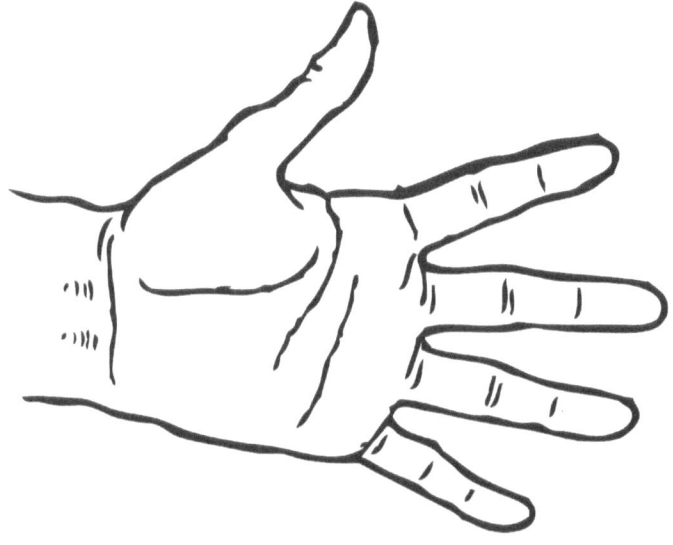

Scripture
Reference_____

Write the passage below:

Research Resources

Insights from second translation or paraphrase:

Key words in their original language with their definitions:

Notes from the commentary:

## Reflection

Why have you chosen to memorize this passage?

_____

_____


What is God saying to you personally through this passage?

_____

_____

_____

_____

_____

_____


In what type of circumstances would knowing this passage
by heart be useful?

_____

_____

_____

_____

_____

## Setting Goals for Memorization

Start Date:

_____

End Date:

_____

Daily Routines to Link to Memorization:

1._____
2._____
3._____

## Memorization Technique

Divide the passage into 5 parts, one part for each finger. Write each portion of the passage beside the finger you will touch when reciting that part of the passage.

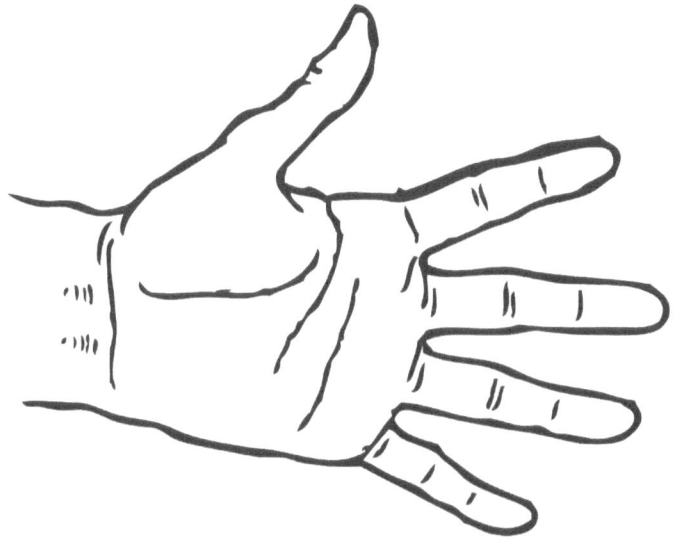

Scripture
Reference_____

Write the passage below:

Research Resources

Insights from second translation or paraphrase:

Key words in their original language with their definitions:

Notes from the commentary:

**Reflection**

Why have you chosen to memorize this passage?

_____
_____

What is God saying to you personally through this passage?

_____
_____
_____
_____
_____
_____

In what type of circumstances would knowing this passage
by heart be useful?

_____
_____
_____
_____
_____

## Setting Goals for Memorization

Start Date:

_____

End Date:

_____

Daily Routines to Link to Memorization:

1._____
2._____
3._____

## Memorization Technique

Divide the passage into 5 parts, one part for each finger. Write each portion of the passage beside the finger you will touch when reciting that part of the passage.

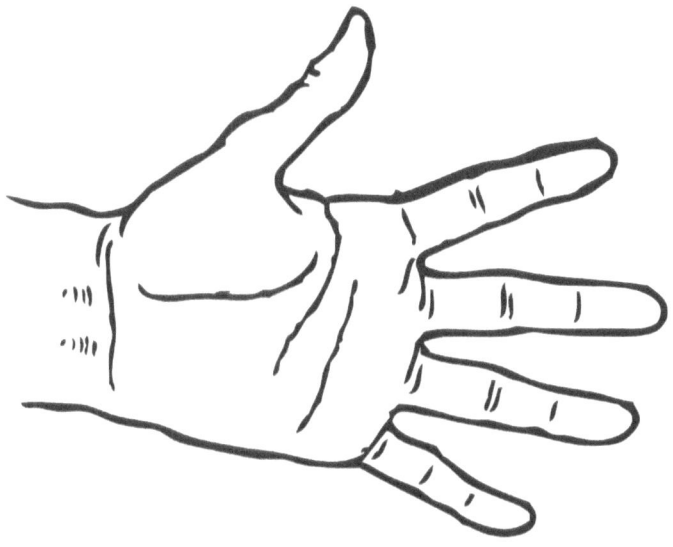

Scripture
Reference_____

Write the passage below:

## Research Resources

Insights from second translation or paraphrase:

Key words in their original language with their definitions:

Notes from the commentary:

## Reflection

Why have you chosen to memorize this passage?

_____
_____

What is God saying to you personally through this passage?

_____
_____
_____
_____
_____
_____

In what type of circumstances would knowing this passage
by heart be useful?

_____
_____
_____
_____
_____

## Setting Goals for Memorization

Start Date:

_____

End Date:

_____

Daily Routines to Link to Memorization:

1._____
2._____
3._____

## Memorization Technique

Divide the passage into 5 parts, one part for each finger. Write each portion of the passage beside the finger you will touch when reciting that part of the passage.

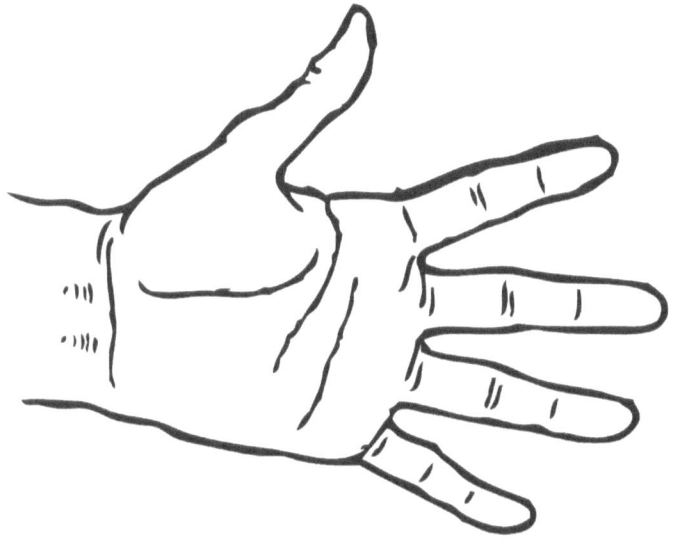

Scripture
Reference_____

Write the passage below:

Research Resources

Insights from second
translation or paraphrase:

Key words in their original
language with their
definitions:

Notes from the commentary:

## Reflection

Why have you chosen to memorize this passage?

_____
_____

What is God saying to you personally through this passage?

_____
_____
_____
_____
_____
_____

In what type of circumstances would knowing this passage
by heart be useful?

_____
_____
_____
_____
_____

## Setting Goals for Memorization

Start Date:

_____

End Date:

_____

Daily Routines to Link to Memorization:

1._____
2._____
3._____

## Memorization Technique

Divide the passage into 5 parts, one part for each finger. Write each portion of the passage beside the finger you will touch when reciting that part of the passage.

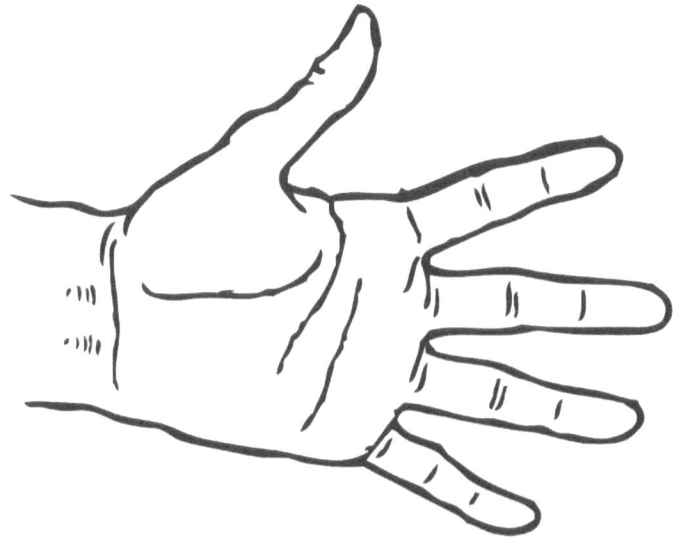

Scripture
Reference_____

Write the passage below:

Research Resources

Insights from second translation or paraphrase:

Key words in their original language with their definitions:

Notes from the commentary:

## Reflection

Why have you chosen to memorize this passage?

_____

_____

What is God saying to you personally through this passage?

_____

_____

_____

_____

_____

_____

_____

In what type of circumstances would knowing this passage
by heart be useful?

_____

_____

_____

_____

_____

## Setting Goals for Memorization

Start Date:

_____

End Date:

_____

Daily Routines to Link to Memorization:

1._____
2._____
3._____

## Memorization Technique

Divide the passage into 5 parts, one part for each finger. Write each portion of the passage beside the finger you will touch when reciting that part of the passage.

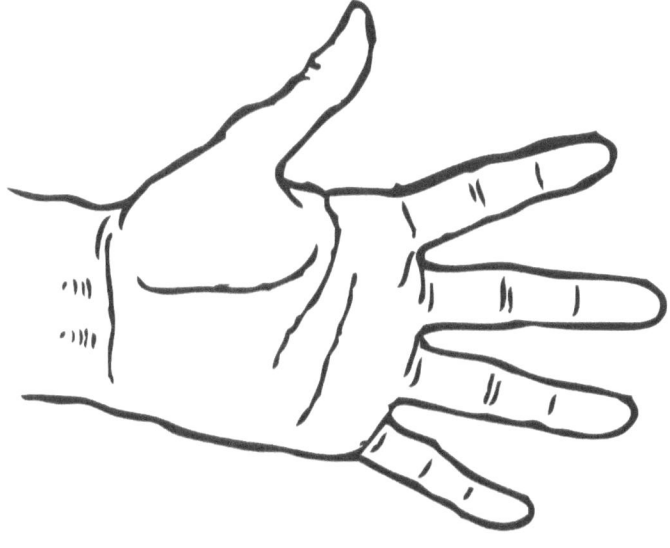

Scripture
Reference_____

Write the passage below:

Research Resources

Insights from second translation or paraphrase:

Key words in their original language with their definitions:

Notes from the commentary:

## Reflection

Why have you chosen to memorize this passage?

_____
_____


What is God saying to you personally through this passage?

_____
_____
_____
_____
_____
_____


In what type of circumstances would knowing this passage
by heart be useful?

_____
_____
_____
_____
_____

## Setting Goals for Memorization

Start Date:

_____

End Date:

_____

Daily Routines to Link to Memorization:

1._____
2._____
3._____

## Memorization Technique

Divide the passage into 5 parts, one part for each finger. Write each portion of the passage beside the finger you will touch when reciting that part of the passage.

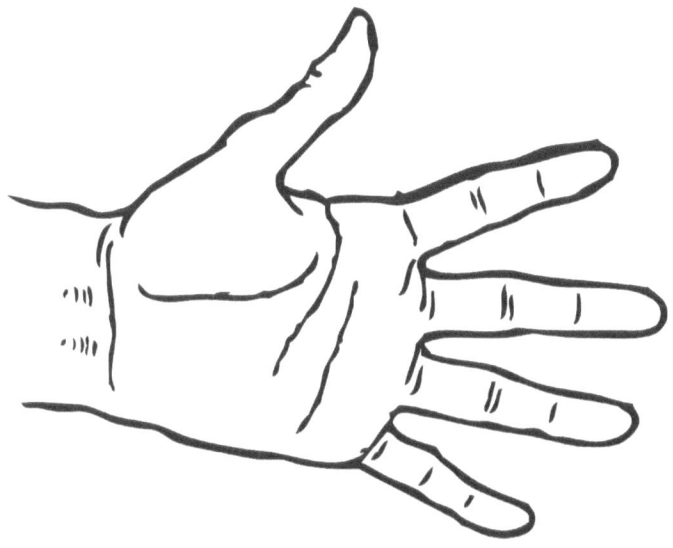

Scripture
Reference_____

Write the passage below:

## Research Resources

Insights from second translation or paraphrase:

Key words in their original language with their definitions:

Notes from the commentary:

**Reflection**

Why have you chosen to memorize this passage?

_____
_____


What is God saying to you personally through this passage?

_____
_____
_____
_____
_____
_____


In what type of circumstances would knowing this passage
by heart be useful?

_____
_____
_____
_____
_____

## Setting Goals for Memorization

Start Date:

_____

End Date:

_____

Daily Routines to Link to Memorization:

1._____
2._____
3._____

## Memorization Technique

Divide the passage into 5 parts, one part for each finger. Write each portion of the passage beside the finger you will touch when reciting that part of the passage.

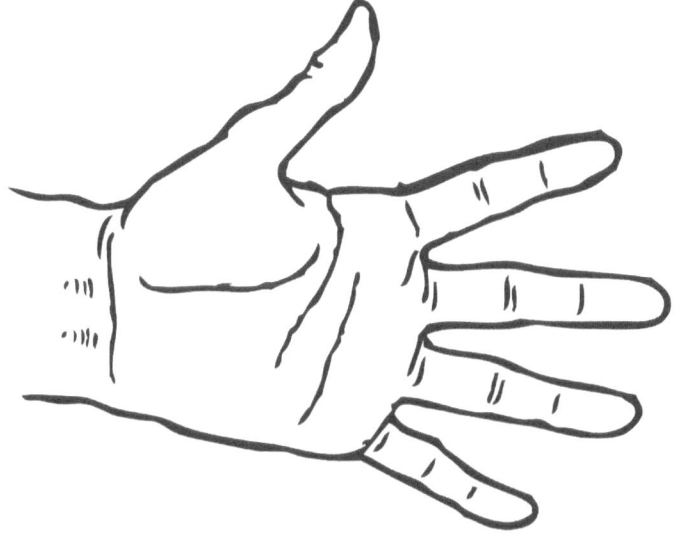

Scripture
Reference_____

Write the passage below:

## Research Resources

Insights from second translation or paraphrase:

Key words in their original language with their definitions:

Notes from the commentary:

## Reflection

Why have you chosen to memorize this passage?

_____

_____


What is God saying to you personally through this passage?

_____

_____

_____

_____

_____

_____

_____


In what type of circumstances would knowing this passage
by heart be useful?

_____

_____

_____

_____

_____

## Setting Goals for Memorization

Start Date:

_____

End Date:

_____

Daily Routines to Link to Memorization:

1._____
2._____
3._____

## Memorization Technique

Divide the passage into 5 parts, one part for each finger. Write each portion of the passage beside the finger you will touch when reciting that part of the passage.

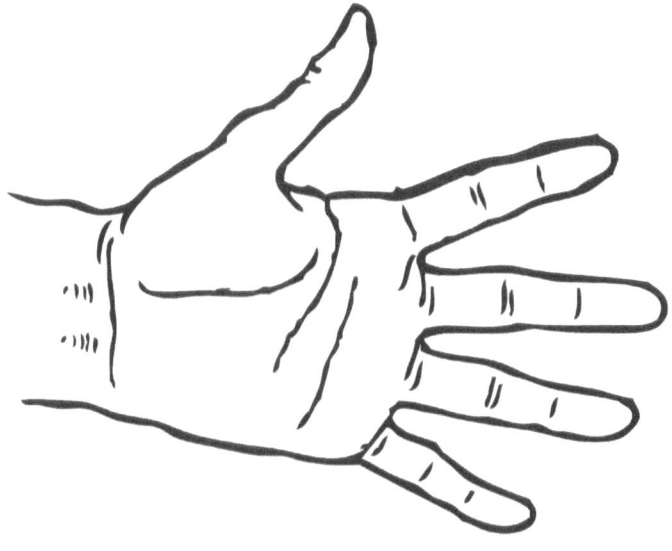

Scripture
Reference_____

Write the passage below:

Research Resources

Insights from second translation or paraphrase:

Key words in their original language with their definitions:

Notes from the commentary:

## Reflection

Why have you chosen to memorize this passage?

_____

_____


What is God saying to you personally through this passage?

_____

_____

_____

_____

_____

_____


In what type of circumstances would knowing this passage
by heart be useful?

_____

_____

_____

_____

_____

## Setting Goals for Memorization

Start Date:

_____

End Date:

_____

Daily Routines to Link to Memorization:

1._____
2._____
3._____

## Memorization Technique

Divide the passage into 5 parts, one part for each finger. Write each portion of the passage beside the finger you will touch when reciting that part of the passage.

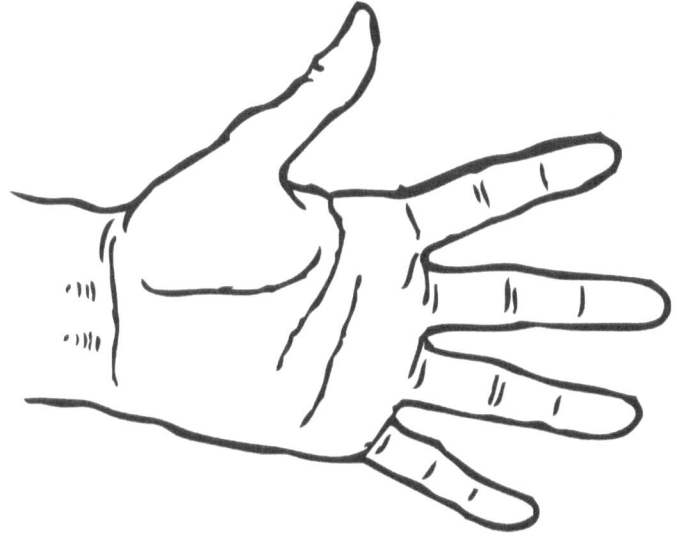

Scripture
Reference_____

Write the passage below:

## Research Resources

Insights from second translation or paraphrase:

Key words in their original language with their definitions:

Notes from the commentary:

## Reflection

Why have you chosen to memorize this passage?

_____

_____


What is God saying to you personally through this passage?

_____

_____

_____

_____

_____

_____

_____


In what type of circumstances would knowing this passage
by heart be useful?

_____

_____

_____

_____

_____

## Setting Goals for Memorization

Start Date:

_____

End Date:

_____

Daily Routines to Link to Memorization:

1._____
2._____
3._____

## Memorization Technique

Divide the passage into 5 parts, one part for each finger. Write each portion of the passage beside the finger you will touch when reciting that part of the passage.

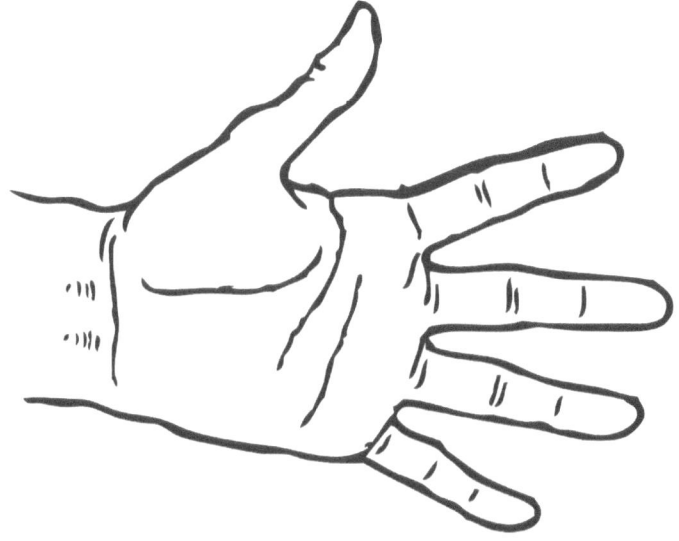

Scripture
Reference_____

Write the passage below:

Research Resources

Insights from second translation or paraphrase:

Key words in their original language with their definitions:

Notes from the commentary:

**Reflection**

Why have you chosen to memorize this passage?

_____
_____

What is God saying to you personally through this passage?

_____
_____
_____
_____
_____
_____

In what type of circumstances would knowing this passage
by heart be useful?

_____
_____
_____
_____

## Setting Goals for Memorization

Start Date:

_____

End Date:

_____

Daily Routines to Link to Memorization:

1._____
2._____
3._____

## Memorization Technique

Divide the passage into 5 parts, one part for each finger. Write each portion of the passage beside the finger you will touch when reciting that part of the passage.

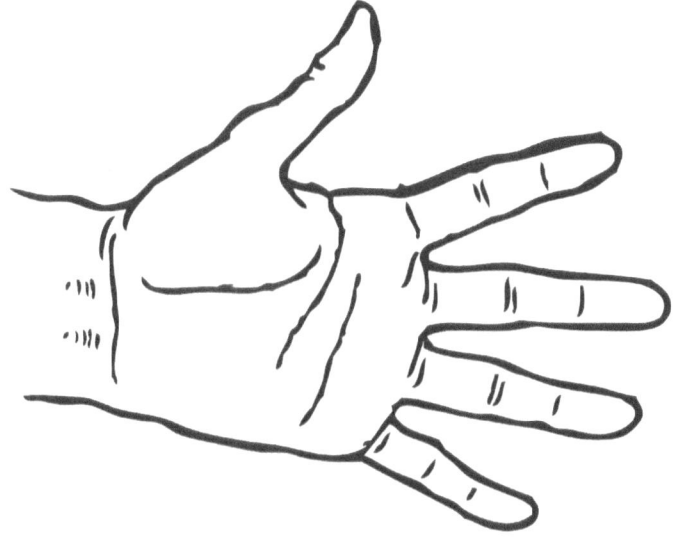

Scripture
Reference_____

Write the passage below:

Research Resources

Insights from second translation or paraphrase:

Key words in their original language with their definitions:

Notes from the commentary:

## Reflection

Why have you chosen to memorize this passage?

_____

_____


What is God saying to you personally through this passage?

_____

_____

_____

_____

_____

_____


In what type of circumstances would knowing this passage
by heart be useful?

_____

_____

_____

_____

## Setting Goals for Memorization

Start Date:

_____

End Date:

_____

Daily Routines to Link to Memorization:

1._____
2._____
3._____

## Memorization Technique

Divide the passage into 5 parts, one part for each finger. Write each portion of the passage beside the finger you will touch when reciting that part of the passage.

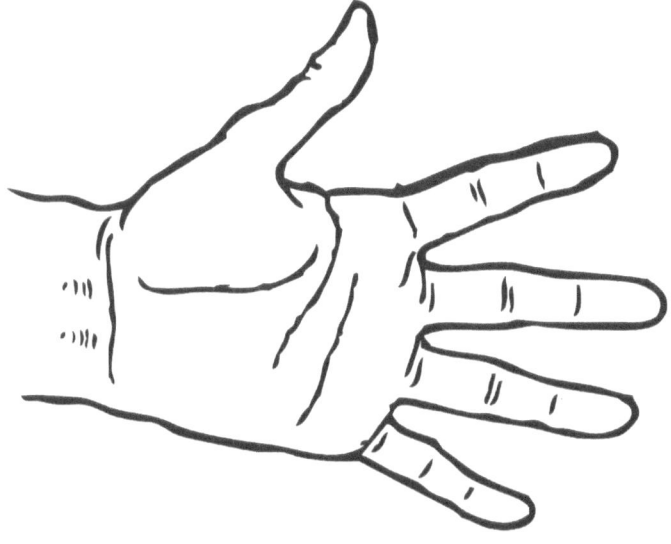

Scripture
Reference_____

Write the passage below:

Research Resources

Insights from second translation or paraphrase:

Key words in their original language with their definitions:

Notes from the commentary:

## Reflection

Why have you chosen to memorize this passage?

_____
_____

What is God saying to you personally through this passage?

_____
_____
_____
_____
_____
_____

In what type of circumstances would knowing this passage
by heart be useful?

_____
_____
_____
_____
_____

## Setting Goals for Memorization

Start Date:

_____

End Date:

_____

Daily Routines to Link to Memorization:

1._____
2._____
3._____

## Memorization Technique

Divide the passage into 5 parts, one part for each finger. Write each portion of the passage beside the finger you will touch when reciting that part of the passage.

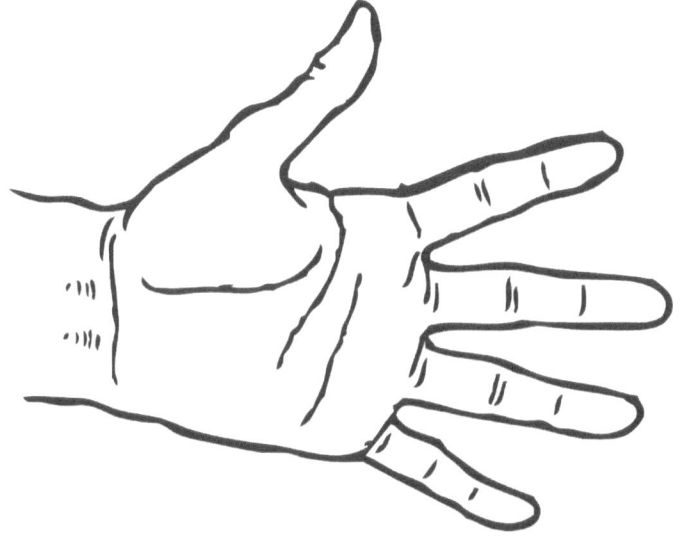

Scripture
Reference_____

Write the passage below:

Research Resources

Insights from second translation or paraphrase:

Key words in their original language with their definitions:

Notes from the commentary:

# Reflection

Why have you chosen to memorize this passage?

_____

_____

What is God saying to you personally through this passage?

_____

_____

_____

_____

_____

_____

_____

In what type of circumstances would knowing this passage
by heart be useful?

_____

_____

_____

_____

_____

## Setting Goals for Memorization

Start Date:

_____

End Date:

_____

Daily Routines to Link to Memorization:

1._____
2._____
3._____

## Memorization Technique

Divide the passage into 5 parts, one part for each finger. Write each portion of the passage beside the finger you will touch when reciting that part of the passage.

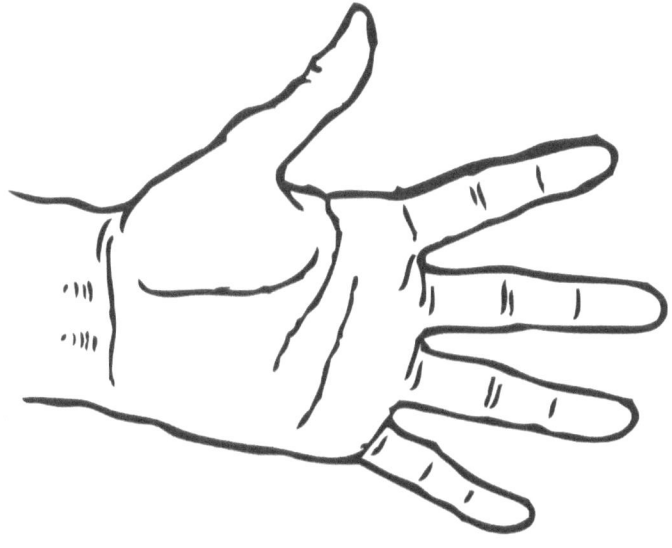

Scripture
Reference_____

Write the passage below:

## Research Resources

Insights from second translation or paraphrase:

Key words in their original language with their definitions:

Notes from the commentary:

## Reflection

Why have you chosen to memorize this passage?

_____

_____

What is God saying to you personally through this passage?

_____

_____

_____

_____

_____

_____

In what type of circumstances would knowing this passage
by heart be useful?

_____

_____

_____

_____

_____

## Setting Goals for Memorization

Start Date:

_____

End Date:

_____

Daily Routines to Link to Memorization:

1._____
2._____
3._____

## Memorization Technique

Divide the passage into 5 parts, one part for each finger. Write each portion of the passage beside the finger you will touch when reciting that part of the passage.

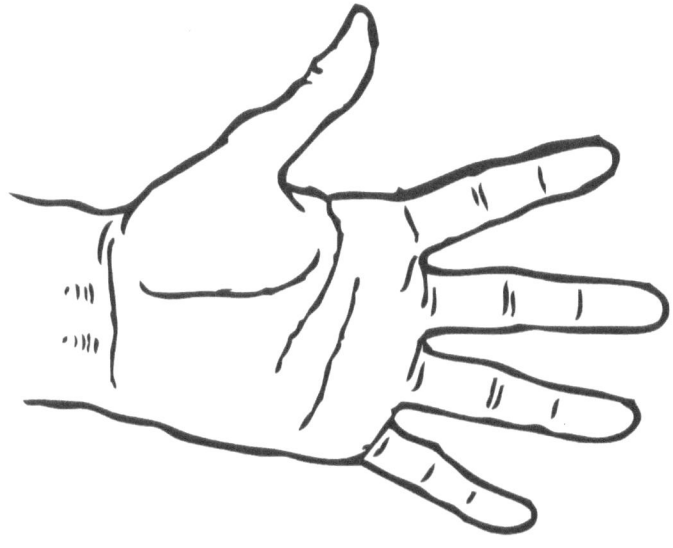

Scripture
Reference_____

Write the passage below:

Research Resources

Insights from second translation or paraphrase:

Key words in their original language with their definitions:

Notes from the commentary:

## Reflection

Why have you chosen to memorize this passage?

_____
_____

What is God saying to you personally through this passage?

_____
_____
_____
_____
_____
_____
_____

In what type of circumstances would knowing this passage
by heart be useful?

_____
_____
_____
_____
_____

## Setting Goals for Memorization

Start Date:

_____

End Date:

_____

Daily Routines to Link to Memorization:

1._____
2._____
3._____

## Memorization Technique

Divide the passage into 5 parts, one part for each finger. Write each portion of the passage beside the finger you will touch when reciting that part of the passage.

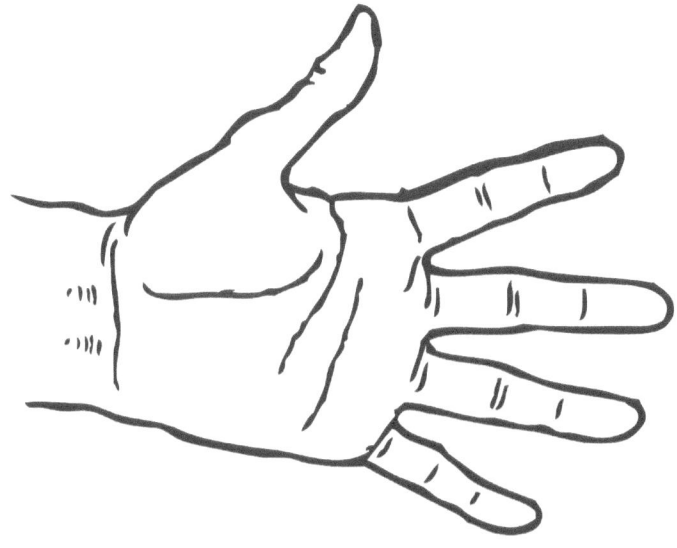

Scripture
Reference_____

Write the passage below:

Research Resources

Insights from second translation or paraphrase:

Key words in their original language with their definitions:

Notes from the commentary:

## Reflection

Why have you chosen to memorize this passage?

_____

_____


What is God saying to you personally through this passage?

_____

_____

_____

_____

_____

_____


In what type of circumstances would knowing this passage
by heart be useful?

_____

_____

_____

_____

## Setting Goals for Memorization

Start Date:

_____

End Date:

_____

Daily Routines to Link to Memorization:

1._____
2._____
3._____

## Memorization Technique

Divide the passage into 5 parts, one part for each finger. Write each portion of the passage beside the finger you will touch when reciting that part of the passage.

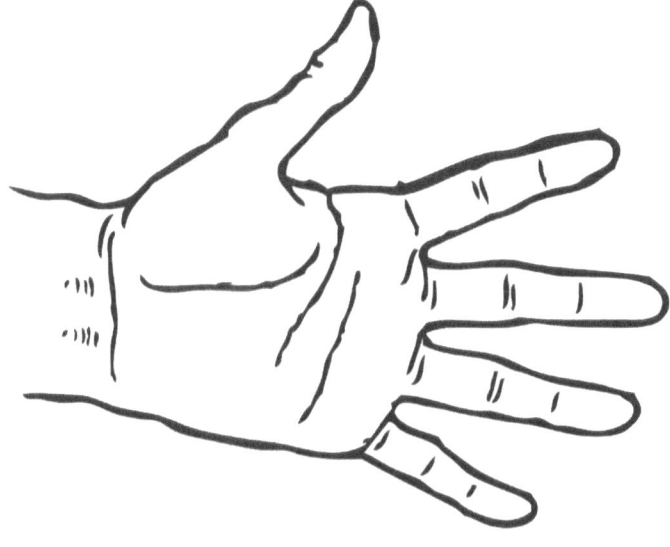

Scripture
Reference_____

Write the passage below:

Research Resources

Insights from second translation or paraphrase:

Key words in their original language with their definitions:

Notes from the commentary:

**Reflection**

Why have you chosen to memorize this passage?

_____

_____


What is God saying to you personally through this passage?

_____

_____

_____

_____

_____

_____


In what type of circumstances would knowing this passage
by heart be useful?

_____

_____

_____

_____

_____

## Setting Goals for Memorization

Start Date:

_____

End Date:

_____

Daily Routines to Link to Memorization:

1._____
2._____
3._____

## Memorization Technique

Divide the passage into 5 parts, one part for each finger. Write each portion of the passage beside the finger you will touch when reciting that part of the passage.

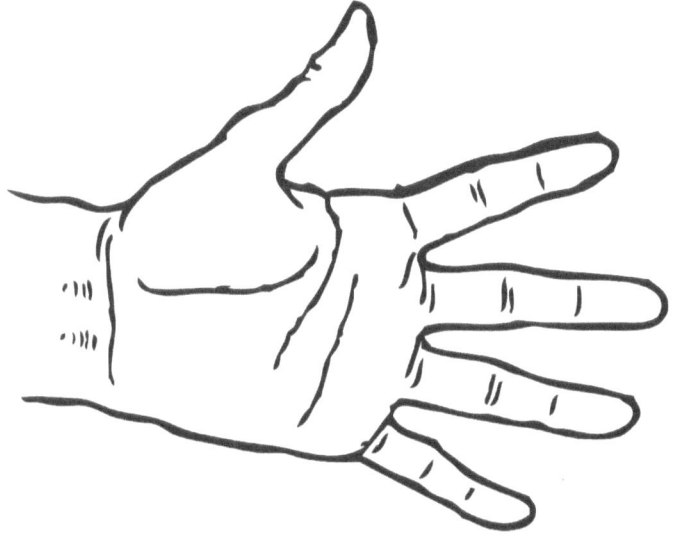

Scripture
Reference_____

Write the passage below:

## Research Resources

Insights from second translation or paraphrase:

Key words in their original language with their definitions:

Notes from the commentary:

## Reflection

Why have you chosen to memorize this passage?

_____

_____

What is God saying to you personally through this passage?

_____

_____

_____

_____

_____

_____

_____

In what type of circumstances would knowing this passage
by heart be useful?

_____

_____

_____

_____

_____

## Setting Goals for Memorization

Start Date:

_____

End Date:

_____

Daily Routines to Link to Memorization:

1._____
2._____
3._____

## Memorization Technique

Divide the passage into 5 parts, one part for each finger. Write each portion of the passage beside the finger you will touch when reciting that part of the passage.

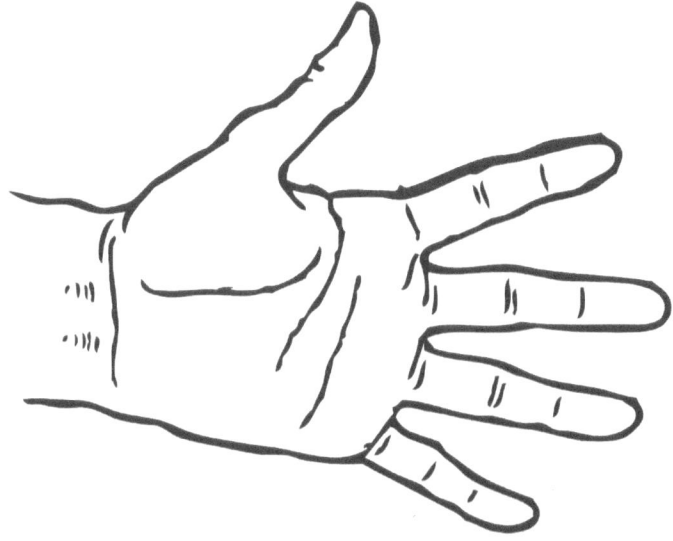

Scripture Reference_____

Write the passage below:

Research Resources

Insights from second translation or paraphrase:

Key words in their original language with their definitions:

Notes from the commentary:

## Reflection

Why have you chosen to memorize this passage?

_____
_____

What is God saying to you personally through this passage?

_____
_____
_____
_____
_____
_____
_____

In what type of circumstances would knowing this passage
by heart be useful?

_____
_____
_____
_____
_____

# Setting Goals for Memorization

Start Date:

_____

End Date:

_____

Daily Routines to Link to Memorization:

1._____
2._____
3._____

## Memorization Technique

Divide the passage into 5 parts, one part for each finger. Write each portion of the passage beside the finger you will touch when reciting that part of the passage.

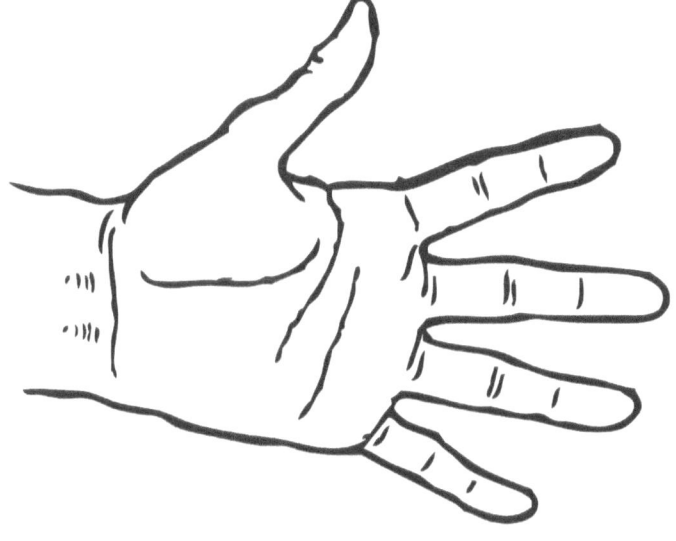

Scripture
Reference_____

Write the passage below:

## Research Resources

Insights from second translation or paraphrase:

Key words in their original language with their definitions:

Notes from the commentary:

## Reflection

Why have you chosen to memorize this passage?

_____

_____


What is God saying to you personally through this passage?

_____

_____

_____

_____

_____

_____

_____


In what type of circumstances would knowing this passage
by heart be useful?

_____

_____

_____

_____

_____

## Setting Goals for Memorization

Start Date:

_____

End Date:

_____

Daily Routines to Link to Memorization:

1._____
2._____
3._____

## Memorization Technique

Divide the passage into 5 parts, one part for each finger. Write each portion of the passage beside the finger you will touch when reciting that part of the passage.

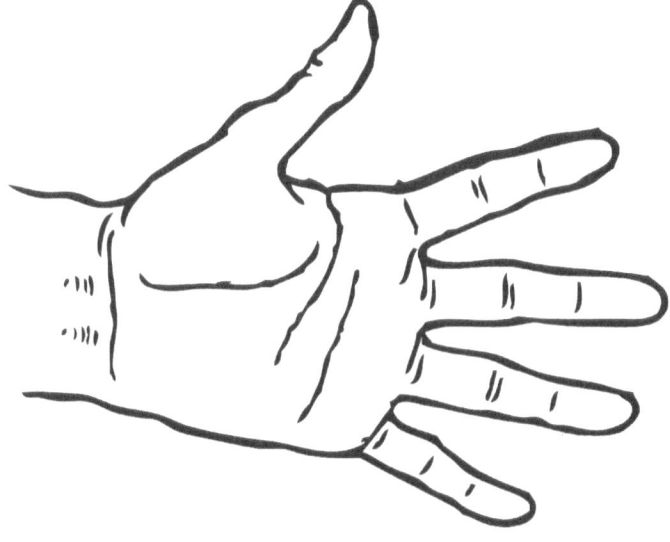

Scripture
Reference_____

Write the passage below:

## Research Resources

Insights from second translation or paraphrase:

Key words in their original language with their definitions:

Notes from the commentary:

## Reflection

Why have you chosen to memorize this passage?

_____

_____

What is God saying to you personally through this passage?

_____

_____

_____

_____

_____

_____

In what type of circumstances would knowing this passage
by heart be useful?

_____

_____

_____

_____

_____

## Setting Goals for Memorization

Start Date:

_____

End Date:

_____

Daily Routines to Link to Memorization:

1._____
2._____
3._____

## Memorization Technique

Divide the passage into 5 parts, one part for each finger. Write each portion of the passage beside the finger you will touch when reciting that part of the passage.

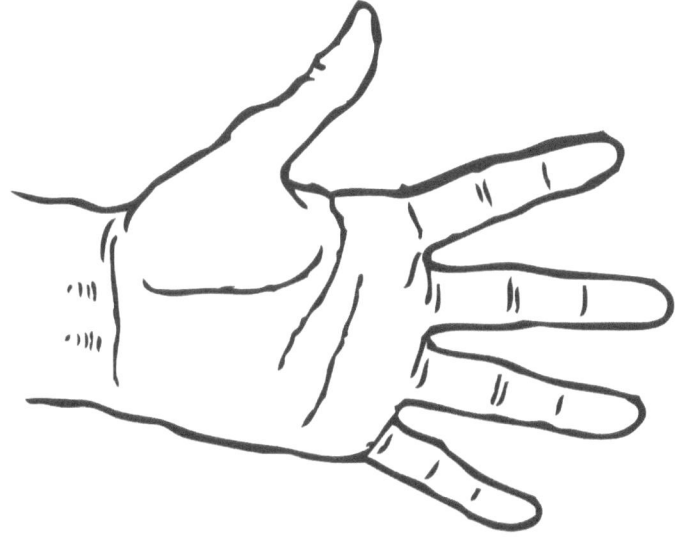

Scripture
Reference_____

Write the passage below:

## Research Resources

**Insights from second translation or paraphrase:**

**Key words in their original language with their definitions:**

**Notes from the commentary:**

## Reflection

Why have you chosen to memorize this passage?

_____

_____


What is God saying to you personally through this passage?

_____

_____

_____

_____

_____

_____

_____


In what type of circumstances would knowing this passage
by heart be useful?

_____

_____

_____

_____

_____

## Setting Goals for Memorization

Start Date:

_____

End Date:

_____

Daily Routines to Link to Memorization:

1._____
2._____
3._____

## Memorization Technique

Divide the passage into 5 parts, one part for each finger. Write each portion of the passage beside the finger you will touch when reciting that part of the passage.

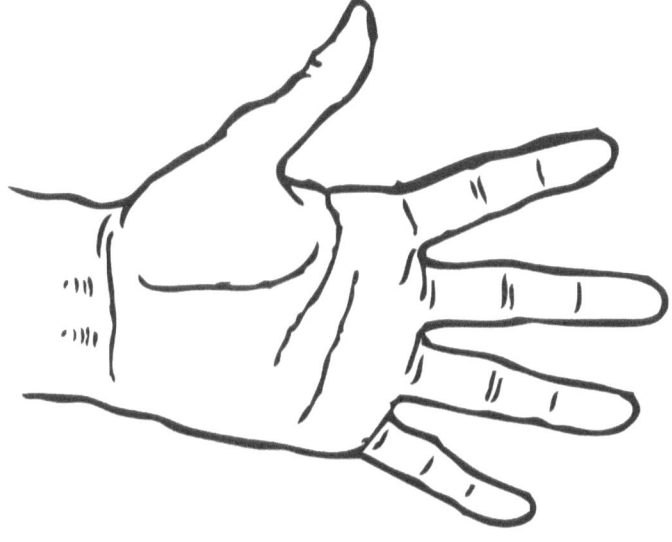

Scripture
Reference_____

Write the passage below:

Research Resources

Insights from second translation or paraphrase:

Key words in their original language with their definitions:

Notes from the commentary:

## Reflection

Why have you chosen to memorize this passage?

_____

_____


What is God saying to you personally through this passage?

_____

_____

_____

_____

_____

_____

_____


In what type of circumstances would knowing this passage
by heart be useful?

_____

_____

_____

_____

_____

## Setting Goals for Memorization

Start Date:

_____

End Date:

_____

Daily Routines to Link to Memorization:

1._____
2._____
3._____

## Memorization Technique

Divide the passage into 5 parts, one part for each finger. Write each portion of the passage beside the finger you will touch when reciting that part of the passage.

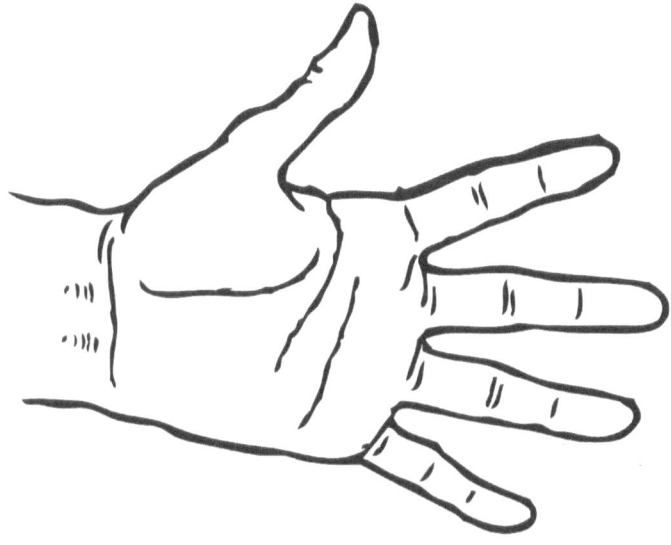

Scripture
Reference_____

Write the passage below:

## Research Resources

Insights from second translation or paraphrase:

Key words in their original language with their definitions:

Notes from the commentary:

# Reflection

Why have you chosen to memorize this passage?

_____
_____

What is God saying to you personally through this passage?

_____
_____
_____
_____
_____
_____
_____

In what type of circumstances would knowing this passage
by heart be useful?

_____
_____
_____
_____
_____

## Setting Goals for Memorization

Start Date:

_____

End Date:

_____

Daily Routines to Link to Memorization:

1._____
2._____
3._____

## Memorization Technique

Divide the passage into 5 parts, one part for each finger. Write each portion of the passage beside the finger you will touch when reciting that part of the passage.

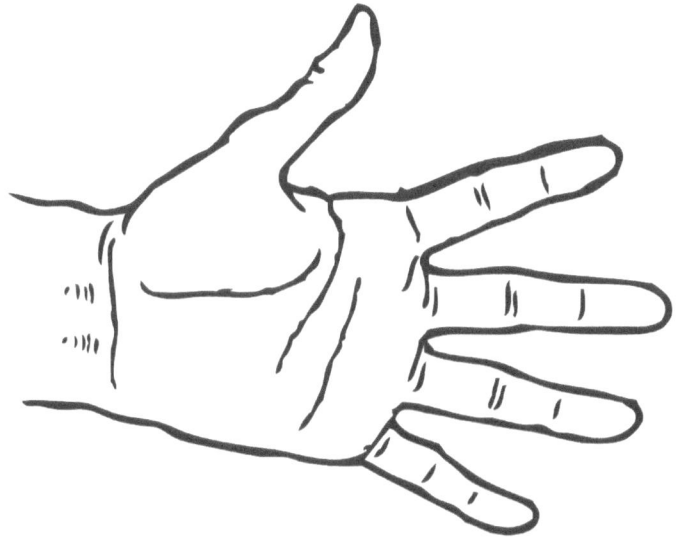

Made in United States
Troutdale, OR
03/03/2025

29459045R00066